Hubert Witheford was born in New Zealand in 1921 and worked as a civil servant in the Prime Minister's Office and other places. In 1953 with his wife and son he moved to England, where he joined the Central Office of Information. After his retirement in 1981 a return to New Zealand proved briefer than he had envisaged.

D0766043

by the same author

SHADOW OF THE FLAME
Pelorus Press, Auckland, 1950

THE FALCON MASK
Pegasus Press, Christchurch, 1951

THE LIGHTNING MAKES A DIFFERENCE
Brookside Press, London, 1962

A NATIVE, PERHAPS BEAUTIFUL
Caxton Press, Christchurch, 1967

HOW DO THINGS HAPPEN?
Flowering Hand Press, London, 1972

A POSSIBLE ORDER
Ravine Press, London, 1980

HUBERT WITHEFORD

A Blue Monkey for
the Tomb

faber and faber
LONDON · BOSTON

First published in 1994
by Faber and Faber Limited
3 Queen Square London WC1N 3AU

Phototypeset by Wilmaset Ltd, Wirral
Printed in England by
Clays Ltd, St Ives plc

All rights reserved

© Hubert Witheford, 1994

Hubert Witheford is hereby identified as the author of this work
in accordance with Section 77 of the Copyright, Designs
and Patents Act 1988.

*This book is sold subject to the condition that it shall not, by way of trade
or otherwise, be lent, resold, hired out or otherwise circulated without the
publisher's prior consent in any form of binding or cover other than that
in which it is published and without a similar condition including
this condition being imposed on the subsequent purchaser.*

A CIP record for this book
is available from the British Library

ISBN 0–571–17012–9

2 4 6 8 10 9 7 5 3 1

Contents

To the Good Lord

I thank You, Lord,
You did not call me
To proclaim in a serious voice
Your ascribed truths,
I would not have had the breath or inclination;

But allow me a while longer
To celebrate Your humorous incarnations
With various numbers of legs –
Romping in Your garden,
Eating each other
If they are economical,
Leaving bits around anyway,

The humans among them
Seeking approval, looking back at the past
And scared of the future.
It is not satisfactory
But it works occasionally.

We rise each morning
Bravely enough. To meet in my case
The little black Burmese
Dancing on her hind legs,
Her voice shrilling from her pink mouth –
An uncanny miniature
Of Your playmate, Kali.

Missing It in 1935

Now and then
I am standing there
On the unwelcome court;

Encouraged thoughtfully
By my parents
Who believed in tennis,

Waiting for the ball
I'd got too tense
To return
Ever.

Of All My Fireworks

Of all my fireworks
'Stromboli'
Was the best.

He was a pyramid
Pyjama-
Striped.

He would start with a putter
As if he was hesitating
To say something

And suddenly
Became an explosion
Of falling lights

And louder
And louder bangs
For a while.

Antipodes

Looking from the veranda
Over the awkward city
We could see the hills almost opposite
And the harbour
Which 'had room for the whole British Navy';

Every day,
I suspect,
My father and mother
Were happier because of it –
That secluded arrangement
Of earth and ocean.

They had the tin roof of our house
Painted green,
Instead of red
Like all the others in Fairlie Terrace.

'You'll be able to find the house
Quite easily.
It's the one with the green roof.'

It makes them sound silly –
But I think they were trying to mitigate
With the means at hand
The insult of mediocrity
To the marvel around them.

Suppose they felt a bit grand
Saying something like that,
How else do I want to feel
Writing this poem?

4 May 1990

Trying to find out
What I feel about the heat
I call it a 'phenomenon'.

What I really mean
Is I don't like it
But am fascinated;

Even the most tolerant
Of dictionaries
Wouldn't encourage that use

Yet all the same
I want the word –
Meaning that something is shown.

And watching
Is more or less the same child
Taken by his mother

Against her better judgement
To a film called *The Lost World*
Where at the end

Dinosaurs
Are incinerated
By volcanoes.

Poseidon

I'll sport no more.

My slaughtered whales
Return in armour-plate
Glowing within them now
The holocaust
And on the ocean floor
The harpoon memory winds

Until they spout.

In the Orongorongos

The only time I heard the bullets
Whistle around my head
Was by a hut called Tawhai.

On the scar
Looking over the valley
We were drinking our beer
And thinking about guerrilla warfare
If the Japs came

When some scum-bag American Marines
Bound for the Solomons
Started shooting at a stag
Rummaging down below.
We flopped down flat.
Later I didn't mind

How many of them
Got back
From Guadalcanal.

Fatality in the Canaries

Considering the naked obese monster
Stumbling across the deck
To accident,
Murder, suicide or natural

Death

Gives us the sort of mystery
We like to read about
And the crude detail
That fleshes it.

Rather more interesting –
When did the story start?
Not, surely, when Goldman Sachs
Phoned they were pulling the plug?

Perhaps when his parents
Were killed – by Nazis
Listening to a demented painter,
Talented, failed in Vienna?

And who sent *him* astray?

It is a tale
Too mean for Sophocles,
A bit much
For Agatha Christie.

November 1991

Arthur Keeps Thinking

Arthur keeps thinking
About what will happen
If he opens his refrigerator
And a two-headed Martian with a ray-gun
Steps out of it.

Arthur has reasons for thinking
That an aggressive visitor
From a desolate and – he has been told –
Technologically advanced planet
Would find his refrigerator a weak point
In the defences
Of our world.

Very few people come to see him now.
He does not go to work any more.
His mother keeps writing long letters to him
And, occasionally,
He is passing blood.

Third World

It is not all that accessible to poetry –
The language
Of a prosperous African
Talking in a South London drawing room
About a future constitution
For his country

That will make human rights
Indisputable.
Next to him
A lightly coloured man
With a sketchy beard
And a dent in his forehead
Is indelibly alert.

His name is 'Captain Hakim – blamed by some
For several assassinations'.
All the time
He is guessing
Where we have hidden
The tape-recorder.

Pub Watching

There are two people sitting between me and the window.
The man is not so much square
As cubic.

The woman slightly negroid,
Attractive.
He says he talks French.

She replies in Creole
To no result.
He explains he is Welsh

And tells her he drank twenty-one pints yesterday.
She nods
In an interested way.

She might be a whore
Or just a very committed
Social worker;

Or perhaps doing no more
Than I am here – waiting
For something to happen.

On Mayne Island,
Remembering Malcolm Lowry

Perfect, the universe
Within my hand:
Lime, salt and ice
Reflect the sun.

But stronger than tequila is the light
The bay gives back,
From rock reverberates
And starts the mind

Born to pin down
Amazement into words,
To freeze
The raven's flight.

The peace you found
Peels like arbutus bark.
The naked boughs remain
In mortal red.

While I Am Waiting

There is an unexpected eeriness
About the butterfly hatching centre —
The pupae are hanging in rows
Some green ones are shivering
They are exciting each other.
I keep coming back to them.

At the other end of the window
Where I looked a moment ago
At a tiny shrivelled sarcophagus
A pair of tiger wings
Have shaken it all off.
They are resting briefly.

Epitaph in Blythburgh Churchyard

I read the stone
And watch the marsh
And fantasize.

Suppose there's dark
And then a candle-flame

After his grasp lets go –
Lets go the wreck
Of being here.

'*Ex umbris*
Et imaginibus
In veritatem.'

Forty years old,
What happened to him?

A Life Together

We want our life
To be like a Persian miniature:
And so, perhaps, it is.

It is like, also,
The strife
Of the chords that are being belted out
By a band
I am drunk enough to enjoy
In an Oriental Bay motel –
The sound
Of one and every other.

Silently

You lift your arms
And lower them.

There is a vaguely electric sound.

Your features are cut more sharply than I remembered
Your upper garment would be tiresome to describe.
Your trousers are green.

I am going now
While you dry your hair.

Breakages

(i)

In the arcade
Our eyes met
Over a wired-up bit
Of porcelain.

(ii)

Later
We had the scent
Of sage
And coriander leaves
As we tore them up.

(iii)

What a pity!
The glass-house
Has been fractured.

It is autumn
And I think our game
Is over.

Spitting Out the Cherry Blossom

Who would have thought that so much pink would do?
They pelt upon my face,
The beauties,
A soft hail storm
On eyes, mouth, cheek.

They won't be anywhere
Next week.
They heap the gutters now.

I've got to breathe,
Love goes too far.
I had not thought
Of petals on my teeth.

Transformations

I'm in the kitchen
Preparing supper
And thinking of a poem about
What happens here.

It might begin

'All the appearances
Inside the room
Emerge perfectly in the instant
They disappear
And are replaced.'

Just after that
Should be some detail
Of the keen terrestrial sort.

I'm fumbling for it

When the top of the liquidizer flies off
And the soup sprays
Everywhere.

Signs

It is more exciting
Before you get there.

According to the guide-book
There are scratches
Made in about fourteen-forty
On the soft plaster
Outside the north wall:

'There seem to be
A lady,
A man, a boat,
And other figures,
With some writing in dog-Latin
It is difficult to translate.'

When you see it
The imagination
Loses its power.
There are just scratches.

Everyday Life in Ancient Assyria

'You can tell,' she said,
'That the people who are hauling up the hill
A Divine Being –
Of about the same size
As the ones at the door of this gallery –
Are not free.

You can tell from their cloth caps
Of a type you could see today
In the Lebanon
Or Israel
They are not Assyrian.

You can see the chains round their ankles
And the men with sticks standing by
Are too close
Not to be ready
To use them.

Not all their faces
Are the same
And a woman who seems to be a captive
Is bending down with a water-skin
For her child to drink from.'

The British Museum, 13.2.87

The Harrowing of Hell in St Mary's, Tillington

What is it he is doing?
Chipped out of ochre stone
A year or so before
The Conqueror came –

With that stark gesture
Of his right hand,
Raising up
Some lolling, hopeless fellow,

And his foot firm
On a sub-terrestrial figure,
Its back rounded
Like a coiled spring.

Why I Have to Look After Them

I do not trust the judgement of the animals.
They are too much involved
As I was
In catching things.

Though they are totally congenial
They are not properly processing
Through their computers
The bytes of danger.

For Him and Her

How dared we intervene
In the lives of two cats
We have presumptuously named
Polo and Cleo?

We got Polo
From a cardboard box
Someone had labelled
'Please look after me?'

Told
He would wander everywhere
Unless he had another animal
At home

We find ourselves now
With a truly feral
Black and orange
Egyptian.

She is not at all well
Which doesn't stop Polo
From exercising himself upon her
Interminably.

We hope only
The vet will be justified
In his subdued optimism
That it is not viral enteritis.

Global Village

Roused by the cats
Even earlier than usual
I turn on the BBC World Service
For encouragement
While opening their tin of Felix,
And get the wailing of dying babies
In Bangladesh.

Cleo steps up her miaouing
And clasps my leg.
Is she sorry for the children?
Or frightened they'll steal her breakfast?
Or is it a purely musical
Participation?

Unsaying

'He has had his thyroid gland honed a little'
A friend just wrote to us about her husband.
She went on to say
'It sounds alarming
But there is absolutely nothing to worry about.'

I kept honing a poem about my parents
Until there was nothing left
But diagnose
Either 'I shy away
From the emotional'

Or 'Life
In its tricky way
Is too dazzling
To talk about
Without deviousness.'

Meeting the animals in their masks
As I come home
They mew supportively
What the Buddha said:

'I have come to the root of the matter
And it proves
Too clear to explain to you.
I'm going to the forest.'

Motif for Poetry

I find myself
Writing a letter
To an unacceptable person

Who is out there
Momentarily
With his furry cap on.

Improbably
There seems more health in him
Than I have known.

It is not to be taken
Seriously
But it should be written.

Cloud-Burst

The fuchsia and I seem happy now.
Up from the sun-hard soil the rain is bouncing
And lightning bursts out of the afternoon.
The radio
Crackles with anger much more lively than the dim
Threats of peace-loving statesmen that it drowns.
Closer
Reverberations. Flower-pots overflow.
Even the heart
Has burst its calyx of anxieties;
The spouting
Cascades superbly into two brown shoes
Put carefully – by someone else – out in the yard.
The lightning makes a difference to the room.

Music for the Night

The wind had risen to storm
But I did not hear the honey-suckle
Beat
On my window-pane.
I was talking too much.

(ii)

Late trains running –
A viable sound
Drowning
The clatter of the mind
I clench to hear.

(iii)

And all the time
Something like a cat
Is purring behind my brain:
I am almost
Stroking its fur.

Swaledale

A lamb is insisting
Successfully
On being fed by its mother
In the middle of the road.

(ii)

Almost into the Swale
Again and yet again
The earthworks of the Brigantes
Obscurely impose themselves.

(iii)

Recurring also
Is information about the Veterinary
And where the Television
Was shot.

(iv)

The boy points at the cage and complains
'Thar's noot even a boodgie';
His father says sombrely
'It's a parrot.'

(v)

And there are too many perfect patterns
Of stone and moor and water
For me to keep on seeing them
Properly.

Interference

It is as though there were someone in a deck-chair
In front of the ocean
Otherwise
Empty until Newfoundland.

I need not walk around
That backside
Of striped colour
To know the mirrored face
That hinders me.

Porthcressa Beach, 7.9.91

Mosquitoes

Images
Of dismay and inconvenience
Hang around me, like a miasma.

Almost the worst things have happened,
They were endurable
And finite.

But this harassment
By petty furies
Of endless loquacity
Goes on and on

Pretending to be a nightmare
Of some low-profile kind
I cannot wake from
And can't destroy me.

All the religions
Have names for it:
'Life'
Seems almost right.

Winter, Autumn, Summer, Spring

AS IT IS NOW

Not much snow on the path.
But it is enough.
I set my feet down
With an apparent
Carefulness.

THE GUY FAWKES GAME

A nest of twigs
Around a flickering.
Then the explosion
Of rotting detritus.
Sparks float through mist.

CLIMBING TO THE MUSEUM

My head swam
In the sun
At Ayios Nikolaos.
Later the Skeleton
In its dolphin sarcophagus.

THE LIMPET HUNTER

Slithering
On the saffron weed
As the tide comes in
I look down
Avidly.

Writing

My hand trembles
It is the vehicle
Of a desire
Not yet clear

Perhaps to decorate
My unreality
Perhaps to be

Not other than
The sunken lane
I walked down yesterday.

Flint under foot
Dry tangle at the side
Green closure
Overhead.

A Blue Monkey for the Tomb

To see the moment
Is its farewell.
Did the Minoan artist of the delicious

Have that in mind
When he painted 'The Saffron Gatherer'
(A blue monkey)

For one departed
Lest joy should fail
In the shadow land?

A memorial
For a man whose name is indecipherable
Gone from this pleasant place.

Miracle

In a front corner
Of *The Miracle at Cana*
A small red dog is rising on its hind legs
To menace
An angry and globular
White cat.

Like the amazed child on their left
And the worried man at his side
We can't but gaze on them.

Knowing what was expected
Boscoli couldn't leave it at that.

There are brightly coloured musicians
Deploying various instruments,
And along the table
A crowd of uneasy guests
Mostly women.

Once you have started to look for Him
You can find among them
A rather insipid chap with a beard
Dressed in white.

Limping

Across the road
I feel the loss of nerve
And acceleration
I had before.

Tottering also
Is the structure
You could call an ego

That was impassable
Until it started
To fall down
Of its own accord.

Going into Winter

I am in the full blast.
Never
I begin to understand
Was I ever
Out of it.

Usually
The trees relax gradually
Into nakedness
But today the leaves hurtle past me.

Each morning
I wake earlier
Mourning
The chances
That will never happen again,

Welcoming
The deluded sparrows
Who think it is dawn.

The World in the Evening

It is a good time to watch the sky.
The clouds
Are not ordinary. They are apricot
Or prussian-blue,
Not vague at all.

Because the sun is setting now
Its obscurations become bright
And look quite solid.

While in the shadow-fall down here
The eroding high-rise flats
Someone imagined for the poor
Are changed as well
To cubic constellations:
As lights are switched on, one by one.

A Poem for My Seventy-First Birthday

It is too late
For almost everything,
A bit too early
Apparently
To wake up.

The dream continues
More and more ominously;
I am not quite convinced by it,
Its colours
Are nearly fading.

Anomalies
I hadn't noticed before
Begin to make it implausible.
What will happen at its stop
Is beyond me.

Now

What seems unlikely to happen
Is a diminishment
Of my anxiety.
It goes on
Depicting scenes in hospital waiting-rooms
That don't quite convince me.

And there's another,
This time totally implausible,
Scenario
At some primitive level of myself
Where Marie is letting the joyful cats in
For ever.

There's an outside possibility
I'll become tired of imaginary futures
And die even further back
Into the unpredictable
Present.

Ekaterinburg, 16 July 1918

I've lost the power
To move at all

Ridiculously I hear
The shoot at Sandringham
More shots to come

Once I was the Tsar
In pheasant time

There's blood all over here
I feel the line of guns
Aim down at me

How to Love Your Life

Floating
In the distance
Now I see it

Like the Town Hall
Tower
At Colchester

Candied extravagance
On brick rectangular.
Alderman Paxman
Paid for it

In nineteen-oh-one
'Out of his own pocket'
Rashly you feel

From across the street.
But descend
To the river

In the misty evening
And then look back —
It is immaterial.
Which master painted it?

A Good View from Holmbury Hill

I wouldn't rely on
Going round that hill again
With the same satisfaction

We had earlier
When we thought we were finding a lost pattern
Of intersecting circles

In the fragmented ditches
Some Celts contrived to defend themselves
And puzzle us.

Too tired for more of that
I look outward
From the amazing repetitions. Free.

What We Have to Do

An expert golfer
Explains it is important
Not to be frightened –

'When you address the ball
Concentrate on the green
Not the adjacent
Lake.'

I realize
It is the lake that has held my attention
All my life.
And what you would expect
Happened.

Our little female cat
Half-saved from starvation
Is similar,
Eats everything
Until she is sick
In case it is taken away.

And yet
The first day she came
From her own Belsen,
Tottering on stick legs,
She found a furry ball on the carpet
And kept throwing it into the air
Again and again and again.